Men Grieve, Too

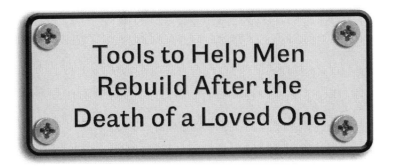

Tools to Help Men Rebuild After the Death of a Loved One

Paul David Madsen

growmedia.com
Omaha, Nebraska

Paperback: 978-0-9713836-5-4

Ebook: 978-0-9713836-2-3

Cover and layout design by Lisa Pelto, ConciergeMarketing.com

Photography by Monica Sempek, MonikaSempekPhotography.com

www.growmedia.com

2916 South 132nd Street #118

Omaha, NE USA 68144

Printed in the United States of America

10 9 8 7 6 5 4 3 2

Contents

Death is personal to me, my sons and my daughter's fiancé. Nine months after the death of my 31-year-old daughter Laura, my wife of 40 years, Lisa, also died. Our family is all-too-familiar with hospice, ICUs, 24/7 oxygen, and all the other things that come with deaths from long-term, chronic illnesses.

When I was 14 years old, my mother, Coral, died of breast cancer. And during my senior year at our tiny high school, my classmates and I mourned the tragic deaths of our friends, Gary and Brad.

Men
Grieve,
Too

Selfishness created this book.

This book started as a journal. Grief counselors and authors tell us to journal and write out our feelings when we lose someone. Well sometimes men keep that "stiff upper lip" and writing out our feelings would be even worse than talking about our feelings. But, more than one person in my life has accused me of being overly expressive, so I ran with that ball and ballpoint pen and started writing. I was writing to help me.

There was no daily journaling or regular, deep thoughts in a pastel-colored diary complete with a sunrise photo on it. I wasn't thinking clearly enough nor disciplined enough to do that kind of writing. No, my scribblings were just random great memories with some anger mixed in now and then, too. This was early on in my losses.

Then I met a woman at my grief group. I'll call her Marge. I hadn't seen Marge at the group before. A grief support group, unfortunately, keeps getting new members all the time. Marge was over 50 years old, and her husband had just died suddenly.

As she told me about the details of his death, she became quite emotional. He died in a location apart from her. She could not stop beating herself up for that. She blamed herself for not being there. It was as if she thought she could have prevented his death if she had just been there. Which, of course, was not true based on her husband's sudden death from natural causes.

After listening well and offering very few words, we shared a hug. She calmed down. She seemed to take comfort from her chat with me. I think it helped her to just say her feelings out loud, to tell her fresh story and to cry about it with someone.

My grief was my focus that day, not someone else's. Yet I found myself accidentally helping someone else through their recent loss. I said nothing heroic nor inspirational to Marge. The fact that I said little was probably the most helpful to her. I was just in the right place at the right time for her. After speaking with her, I realized it—comforting Marge comforted me. I wanted more of that!

When I later pondered how I could help more people like Marge, I considered turning my journaling into a book about grief. What the heck, I already had some scribbled ramblings, and I own a "qualifying story." But after a brief search online, I realized the world does not need yet one more book about grief.

But then came another realization: Most of the folks at the various grief groups I've attended were women. Why aren't there more men? And the guys who attend these groups tended to stay quieter than the females. Why?

Is it because guys are taught from a young age to keep that "stiff upper lip?" Did macho actor John Wayne get to us through our fathers, grandpas and uncles? This book is not a psychological research paper on the differences between men and women, nor is it a study of the culturalization of men. Nor is it a sensitivity class for men. It is simply an exercise to help guys sort out where we are headed and to track things after terrible events in our lives.

Men Grieve, Too can help you get a feel for where you are mentally, emotionally and spiritually after the loss of your loved one. Since guys tend to not say very much, perhaps this material will help us to quietly appraise or measure our status. It can be a grief tool we can hold in our hands to do the work of grief. Most guys like tools. I've included tool imagery in each of the chapters about types of male grief to serve as daily reminders for us on our grief journeys.

I've done career coaching with professionals for decades. I gave corporate IT and health care professionals the tools they needed to advance their careers. This book evolved from that work; as a tool to help myself and other grieving men. It is intended to help us sharpen our saws in the face of grief. Chapters about male types of mourning come with a symbolic tool image to keep in mind during our daily grief journeys.

But what about women? Women grieve and deserve just as much attention, help and support as men when they lose a loved one. In some cases, women have more difficult grief journeys than men. They may be more negatively affected financially, socially and in other ways by the deaths of their loved ones.

My heart goes out to all who have lost loved ones. However, this book is for men. By a man and for men. A book about antique motorcycles is different from a book about antique bicycles.

While both are typically two-wheeled modes of transportation, their titles and content have to be different. The same goes for this book. Women grieve and men grieve. However, this book is focused on men's grief. It comes out of research and my personal experiences.

The content of types of male mourning—Sweepers, Weepers, Sheepers, Leapers and Keepers—is based on anecdotal, not empirical research. I read numerous books on grief and read parts of many more. I consumed scores of podcasts and videos on the topic. I had many interviews with other grieving people, plus a good number of discussions with professionals who work around death and dying. I've attended numerous grief group events, seminars and even social events comprised of people in mourning. And, of course, I'm still working on my own grief journeys.

So, let's get to it guys. You've been forced into taking this terrible trip. What entrance and exit ramps will you take or avoid? If you'll consider slowing to ask for directions, maybe we can navigate this thing together.

Chapter 1

"Keep a Stiff Upper Lip!"

That's a classic "man to man" line often used with regard to emotion. The Cambridge Dictionary says, "Someone who has a stiff upper lip does not show their feelings when they are upset." The idiom has roots in Britain and encourages one to remain resolute by not letting a trembling lip demonstrate fear.

Men are sometimes told, or they culturally learn, to think they should keep a stiff upper lip in the face of death. For a variety of reasons, some men won't show grief or accept much help with their mourning. Perhaps this comes from the fictitious "John Wayne School of Grieving."

Hollywood actor John Wayne starred in 141 cowboy and military movies up to 1975. He was the epitome of toughness. Of macho. He was a man who perhaps influenced a generation of grandpas, dads, uncles, brothers, coaches and leaders. My favorite John Wayne movie is "True Grit." Perhaps a more modern Hollywood example is the somewhat emotionally distant Vin Diesel who has starred in many of his own testosterone-filled action movies.

A couple of John's quotes:

"Talk low, talk slow and don't say too much."

*"Never apologize and never explain
—it's a sign of weakness."*

Many guys have a little John Wayne in them when it comes to showing emotions. We clam up and say very little sometimes. We just tough it out. Especially relating to death. That can also apply to men who want or need to give emotional support to others. We don't say too much.

But men do grieve. Despite a culture where men are sometimes expected to not show too much emotion, men still hurt when loss occurs. They may grieve differently than women. They may grieve differently than other men. They grieve in their own way. This book is to help all mourning males to simply be aware of a variety of pathways a guy may take in his grief journey.

Generally speaking, guys lean toward the "quantitative." We like to check the oil in our cars, know our miles-per-gallon, memorize statistics on our sports teams and athletes, tweak machines to maximum efficiency, know exactly how long it takes to get somewhere, follow our investment returns closely, know the square footage of our home, remember class sizes, scores, populations and ranks. Most of us like to *track stuff.* Are we born with a "quantification gene?" In many cases, it appears to be true.

Tracking (being aware of) types of male mourning may help us measure where we are after our loss. It might give us a tiny hint of control during a time when we feel so out of control. So, what is a "Type of Male Mourning?"

A "Type of Male Mourning" is just a handle. Are you old enough to remember the word "handle" from the 1970s CB (Citizens' Band) radio craze? CB radio culture had a jargon of its own. "What's your handle?" was a request for your nickname identity. CB radio users also asked, "What's your 20?" which was a request for your location.

CB radio jargon is similar to Types of Male Mourning because these Types name and locate our grief in a way. Naming and locating our status may help us get a grip on our grief trip. Here are five Types of Male Mourning:

Sweepers

Weepers

Sheepers

Leapers

Keepers

I've experienced all of these Types of Male Mourning and I'm still experiencing some of them. There are probably other types of grief and mourning as well. Your grief will look different from the next guy's and from mine. Hopefully discussing these Types of Male Mourning will help you "find your 20."

Types of Male Mourning are not steps you will take or phases you go through. They are not stages or a "process." They are not in any order. Some men will experience none of these and some may experience more than one of them at the same time. There is no one road map you are supposed to follow. Your grief is just that—yours.

If you identify with one or more of these Types, great. If not, that is OK, too. One of the Types describes positivity and a hint of peace. It may be an ultimate goal in your grief journey, or you may not get there. You decide where you are and where you fit. No matter what that is, trust that it is right for you.

The lighthearted handles I use for male grievers are in no way intended to diminish the serious impact of death. These titles are simply mnemonics—a writing device/tool to help us remember things. God knows our brains are already under stress. The Type names are about keeping things easy.

The Oxford Dictionary's definitions of grief and mourning:

Grief: "A deep sorrow, especially that caused by someone's death."

Mourning: "The expression of deep sorrow for someone who has died, typically involving following certain conventions such as wearing black clothes."

All of us who've lost someone special know that grief and mourning go way beyond those descriptions. Grief is all encompassing. The slight difference between the definitions is mostly about "the expression" of sorrow. Both meanings connote deep sadness after loss or death. This book uses the words "grief" and "mourning" interchangeably.

The following chapters illustrate 5 Types of Male Mourning for you to ponder.

Chapter 2

Sweepers

"I'll be OK"

Steve:

"Yes, Sheryl and I were married for 35 years. She's gone now. Cancer is a terrible thing. I hate how she suffered at the end. Nobody deserves that. Fortunately, I still have a nice family and a couple of cute grandkids. I have lots of great memories of Sheryl, but nothing I can do will bring her back. She's in a better place, so that's all we need to worry about.

"I'm OK and I don't want to talk about it for God's sake! She's gone, so why do people want to keep bringing her up? I've got a lot of other important things to do and I'm staying busy so let's just move forward here. Let's let her rest in peace."

Cliff:

"That accident never should have happened. Why did Maddie try driving in that weather? She was an inexperienced driver. I told her on the phone to stay put at school until the snowplows got around. I'll always miss her, but she's gone. I'm sad about it but I'm not going to cry about it every day. I cried hard at the visitation and at the funeral. But I don't want everyone to keep reminding me about it because it just makes me sad.

"I've got a life to live and need to provide for the rest of my family. My job will be demanding again soon. They have given me space for a while. There are lots of medical bills to pay so I have to keep the boss happy and stay employed. Some of you seem like you can just sit around and mope most of the time. That's not a luxury that I have. Damn that blizzard!"

***

A cousin to keeping a stiff upper lip, sweeping things under the rug is an idiom that refers to someone who is sweeping a floor and is left with that pesky bit of dust that never seems to go into the dustpan. The solution is to lift up the corner of a freestanding rug and sweep the dust under there and out of sight. The dust is magically gone! The problem is out of sight. And out of mind. Forever, right?

The corollary with death is, of course, that when Sweepers are faced with the death of someone close to us, we sometimes sweep our emotions under the rug. The clinical word for that is denial. But John Wayne students don't admit to denying anything. We just face the problem, process it and maybe ignore it. We deal with it and move on thinking that there's nothing to see here.

Men see themselves as leaders and as tough and we have to keep things under control. Someone has to be in charge here, right? We can power through this. You know the phrases: *Rub some dirt on it. Walk it off. Toughens you up.*

These are valid concepts of who we may be some of the time. Perhaps more so during/around/after death. This is not necessarily wrong and we hope nobody is trying to change us. We are who we are, *Pilgrim*. So there. Sweepers suppress grief. We ignore it. We sweep it under the rug.

Do you know why we do this?
It's easier!

It is much easier to ignore the pain than to deal with it. The pain of loss doesn't go away, but the amount of attention and focus we give it *is* controllable.

For our family's funerals, we made huge bulletin boards with hundreds of photographs from family life with my wife and daughter. For over a year after our daughter's death the boards were still on display in our main dining area. Two boards really—one for Laura and one for Lisa. I loved looking at them and the memories that were so clear from each and every emotional photograph. Moments of tears came often.

Those displays may not seem like a "Sweeper" activity. We enjoyed displaying and loving all those memorable photos. While it's true that the lingering of the displays by themselves is not really a Sweeper activity, it was time to take them down or at least reduce their prevalence. However, I kept sweeping *that* task under the rug.

"If I take these pictures down and put them out of sight, doesn't that mean I'm forgetting about their lives and all those memories? No, I'll just sweep that task under the rug and let those boards stay right where they are, thank you very much. What's wrong with keeping a shrine in place? They aren't hurting anything!"

It was easier to leave them up and I did. But I'm glad to tell you that as a result of writing this chapter I've reduced those picture boards to two prominent portraits. Shrine reduction is now complete.

Regarding the avoidance of grief, I've heard this from several sources:

Even if you sweep it under the rug, grief will find you.

How has sweeping your grief under a rug worked out for you? Have you found yourself being angry in ways you weren't before? I got a big laugh from a grief group when the leader asked us if we were more angry than usual. My reply: "I've noticed since the funerals that there are a lot more bad drivers out there!" So, I guess, yes, some anger lies below my surface. How about you?

Is it hard to concentrate? Are you sad about things that never used to make you sad? Have you changed your social behaviors other than the obvious ones of not maintaining the routines you had with your loved one? These could all be symptoms of a Sweeper Type. And guess what?

These are normal. These are expected. Especially for Sweepers.

Remember that being a Sweeper is okay and normal... there's nothing wrong with having Sweeper-type tendencies while on your grief trip. We may simply be acting and feeling like other men in our lives do or did when faced with a highly emotional situation.

Sweeping things under the rug has been normal for millions of men...especially some of the Greatest Generation and their Baby Boomer offspring. I've heard stories about men who came back from their service in World War II, Korea, and Vietnam who went on to say *nothing* about their war-time experiences.

Think of the carnage they experienced and then they lived out the rest of their civilian lives *not* talking about that. If that's what they did, they certainly swept a lot under the rug. The Post-Traumatic Stress Disorder (PTSD) that many experienced, diagnosed or undiagnosed, after war could be that grief coming back and finding them.

Within the last few decades, it seems that younger men are more open to verbalizing their grief. This includes grief from war experiences in the Middle East or from personal losses.

Generations X, Y and Z and Millennials born after the Baby Boomers are changing the landscape. John Wayne is long dead. And millions of younger men are not as likely to be Sweepers as their fathers were. This is a good thing.

∗∗∗

A tool imagery for a Sweeper is a sanding block. This is a piece of wood, rubber or plastic that fits into your hand. The flat side of the block holds sandpaper in place and the operator moves it over the wood which needs sanding.

When woodworkers make cuts in wood there are often rough edges which need to be sanded and smoothed to ensure proper fit and appearance. Wood is originally cut into about the size which is needed but high-touch sanding perfects the piece.

A dear friend creates amazing artistic clocks made of 100% wood. They are beautiful kinetic sculptures which happen to tell time. He brings wood to life via the movement of these artistic pieces. As you might guess, he's spent much of his life sanding thousands of wood parts into the proper shapes and sizes. His awe-inspiring works remind me of what sanding can do to reshape something and bring out its beauty. It can make even a gnarly, perhaps unattractive piece of wood into a functional, precise and pleasing piece.

Sweepers can use that imagery to heal. Sanding wood smooths it and customizes it so it fits into its artistic or functional spot. Our lives are masterpieces in the making in God's eyes even amidst raucous grief. Will you allow yourself to be sanded, molded and formed into a functional piece?

If you have a tendency to sweep your grief under the rug, consider placing a small sanding block where you'll see it every day. It can be a reminder that the rough edges of our grief can slowly and eventually be sanded off, bit by bit or layer by layer.

If you don't have or want a sanding block, then consider a wooden item that was important to you and your loved one. Perhaps your table where you ate or how about a favorite desk or wooden chair you both loved? Or even your bed's headboard. Most wooden items required significant sanding before becoming a final product in your home.

We can emotionally attach a "sanding block reminder" to that item by simply tapping it each day. This might remind us that mourning men are works in progress. Yes, we are a mess right now, but we still have potential for a smoother future. Sweepers have rough surfaces, but with sanding, that coarseness is not permanent.

Here's your chance to help other Sweepers.

What advice do you have for Steve?

How about Cliff? What would you tell him?

Are YOU a Sweeper?

Yes_____No_____ Maybe_____

If you answered yes or maybe to the above, what actions imply that you may be or have been a **Sweeper?**

Grief is not permanent. While our sadness over loss may linger forever, I've seen the intensity of that change over time. Since many men like to quantify and measure stuff, the tool below can help you measure how you are feeling "today" as you deal with your loss. It can help you to know if your Sweeper tendencies, if you have any, are static or changing. Consider coming back to this page in 3, 6 and 12 months for reflection. If you agree to do this, put reminders on your phone or calendar now.

Yes. Right. Now.

My Sweeper thoughts 3 months from my original reading of this chapter Month___Year___

My Sweeper thoughts 6 months from my original reading of this chapter: Month___Year___

My Sweeper thoughts 12 months from my original reading of this chapter: Month___Year___

Peace to all Sweepers!

Chapter 3

Weepers

"I just feel like crying all the time."

Craig:

"I have no energy. That funeral week wiped me out. So many people and relatives. Some I haven't seen in decades including a few I haven't seen since Sandy and I got married. The nerve of Uncle Jerry showing up to the funeral and acting like he was all close to us after what he has been like for decades! People like that stress me out.

"Everyone's gone now and the food gifts from people have stopped coming. That's OK because I can't keep up with thanking people for all the nice things they have done. But I'm so sad and lonely. It's so quiet around here. I don't really cry; I just *feel* like crying all the time.

"There's such a hole in my life! We were just getting ready to enjoy the good life. I have to cancel those reservations for that Alaskan cruise and I need to find out where Sandy put the reservation for our resort cabin for our summer trip. Ugh! Sandy, where do you keep this stuff?

"I'm glad I'm retired because I can't even imagine going to work. I feel like I can't go out in public like this.

If I do, all I see are places and things that remind me of Sandy and I feel like crying *again*. I'm tired of feeling like this all the time. It feels like there's a weight on my chest. When will this end? Why did you leave me? I'm not sure I can go on or if there's any reason to!"

∗∗∗

Jermaine:

"They've been really nice to me at work since my dad and mom died so closely together. Dad was my best friend and we had so many projects we had planned to do together. We were ready to buy that cabin and fix it up after he retired. It would have been perfect for family retreats after Dad and I did our magic. He was going to do most of the work since he was retiring. He had all the carpentry skills we needed. I sure don't have all that. I was going to rely on him! He had so much talent and he was the leader for this family. Now everyone is going to look to me to be the strong one. But that's a joke since I'm just deeply sad all the time.

"At work I just stare at my computer screen and do nothing but sniffle and think about what might have been. I would have loved the family holidays we could have done at the lake after Dad did his thing. This grief thing really has me losing hope about life in general. What's the point anymore? We always knew Mom's days were numbered due to her health but Dad surprised us all and nearly followed her right up to Heaven! He was pretty healthy; but the stress of losing his soulmate was too much on his heart.

"They're going to say something about my work, or lack of it, pretty soon. I know others on my team are carrying me. But I just can't concentrate or think of anything but the big hole I feel like I'm in. Losing them both dominates my thoughts. All the plans we had! My life as I had hoped and planned for it is now gone in an instant. Poof! I suppose I should try to look busy... But why? I really just don't care anymore."

* * *

A few cultures and religions around the world utilize professional Weepers. Their use varies from place to place based on belief systems. Locations where they are used include parts of China, Egypt and Europe. Some professional Weepers are hired like actors to attend funerals and play the part of being sad. They are cast as "extras" so to speak—no speaking parts except for perhaps a standard courtesy offered in a receiving line to the family who lost a loved one.

The departed's family or the funeral arrangers hire these professional Weepers in order to make it look like the dead person had lots of friends and was well-loved. Similar to paying for "likes" or followers on social media-spending money to appear popular.

Some hired Weepers wail, moan, cry and/or sing loudly at funerals and funeral related events. They raucously take on and display the grief of the family who has a dead loved one. Their role is to make a big scene and spread the collective pain.

Now you are aware that there are people in the world who are professionally known as Weepers. Those aren't the Weepers we are talking about here. Craig and Jermaine above are different kinds of weepers. They are men who feel like the loss of their loved one is a black hole they just can't crawl out of. Ever. That makes them sad.

Like most of us, Weepers can't imagine life without our loved one. If we lost a child, a young adult offspring, a parent or a wife, all we know is that life is not the same and never will be again. It is not a life that we know or want to know. It all seems meaningless. We want our *old* lives back! We are in maximum mourning because we lost what we had and what we hoped for and visualized in the future. A double loss—present companionship is now gone *and* our dreams for the future have now vanished too.

Maybe that hope was a mob of grandkids posing with you and your bride by the Christmas tree for the perfect-looking Christmas card photos. Maybe it would have been the family gathered at the lake house rental every Fourth of July. Whatever the scenario, it won't happen now. A hole exists in place of all hope and anticipation.

That's depressing.

We feel so sad, alone and despondent. There seems to be no point to much of anything. Especially if, like Craig, our loss was a spouse with whom we were just getting ready to enjoy the good life. Like Jermaine, all our plans and visions for the future have vaporized. That makes us sad. Or beyond sad. It makes us want to give up altogether. Everything has changed.

I've read that there are up to seven types of depression. This book is not about depression, however, that topic is relevant to any discussion of grief. The following is a light treatment of two main types of depression and how they relate to mourning men.

Regarding depression, please utilize qualified professionals to learn more.

Clinical Depression, according to WebMD.com, is what is occurring when the brain is not operating properly and this interferes with the daily function of a person. It shows itself in several types of physical manifestations and behavior changes. The most severe is when a person wants to take his (or her) own life *and makes plans* or attempts to do so. **If that is you or someone you know, get professional help. Now.**

For immediate professional

help or intervention, contact:

The National Suicide Prevention Lifeline:

800-273-8255

or online:

www.suicideprevention.org

* * *

Situational Depression/Adjustment Disorder is just what it sounds like. According to Betterhelp.com, a change like the death of a loved one is the trigger for symptoms that include the following:

- Feeling sad and crying frequently
- Listlessness
- Feeling hopeless and helpless
- Losing interest in things you used to enjoy
- Feeling worried or jittery
- Having trouble sleeping
- Problems concentrating
- Losing your appetite
- Feeling overwhelmed
- Impaired daily functioning
- Withdrawing from your support system
- Avoiding things that seem hard, like going to work
- Suicidal thoughts

Many of those symptoms accompany raw, new grief in most men. I have felt many of them. I read in several sources, how these symptoms of situational depression are all normal for grieving guys. But normal or not, it still doesn't make us feel better. We just want it to be over.

I discuss depression because I see it in fellow grievers. Those observations plus my personal experiences conclude that Situational Depression is typical and for those of us who have lost loved ones.

Here's my view of that:

My daughter and my wife died 9 months apart. I have found myself grieving "differently" for my daughter than for my wife. Not harder or better or worse for one or the other... just differently and at a different pace of grieving with each of them. My grief and mild depression are situational.

* * *

I know guys; it's the last thing you want to hear right now. You don't want to hear that these things are situational because you have a raw, gaping wound left by the death of your loved one. You don't need some cheerleader telling you this is all normal, everything is situational and "this too shall pass." You are hurting and don't want to hear it. Been there. Doing that. It is OK to feel depressed and sad.

The deaths of my loved ones are still fairly new so I'm not sure I can tell you from experience that Situational Depression goes away. However, I've visited with other male mourners who are further out from their loss than I am. They say or seem like the depression surrounding the situation does, in fact, slowly fade. We, of course, never forget our loved ones. Do we just eventually "get used" to the pain and that big hole in our lives? The answer may be yes.

* * *

> **One way to deal with your inner Weeper is to consider taking a break from your constant, overwhelming grief. What I mean is to decide to take "time off" from your pain.**

"I can't control this stuff," you protest. But maybe you can. Think about when you went on a family vacation in the good old days. You had/have a job that consumed you, however you knew you were getting time off from July 4th through the 11th for your big trip.

You planned and planned to be able to go on this trip without any remorse or distractions. You covered all bases and were going to be able to leave work behind (smart phone and all) for some precious, work-free days with your family.

Smartphones put a damper on our ability to ever totally separate from work, but you know the drill. You were thrilled with the idea of several days out of the workplace and a chance to spend time with your family. You worked hard to put your stakes in the ground to block out your space.

You compartmentalized. You organized your thinking to be able to stop your brain's focus on your workplace. You were able (mostly) to be with your family and separate yourself from your work life. Your spouse was impressed how you were able to leave your smartphone in the car and not take it to the beach or on the jet ski with you.

**Did you quit your job to make this trip? No.
Did you stop caring about your employer or
business to make this trip? No.
But yet you pulled out for a week, didn't you?
You were able to keep your job and also enjoy
your family.**

How about doing that with your grief? If you try this it doesn't mean that you quit your grief or that you are done grieving. You won't stop caring about your loss. You won't forget about your loved one. But can you give yourself permission to hit the pause button on your grief just for *one hour*? You pulled out of your workplace's mental grind for a week—how about a vacation from your grief for just an hour? Or maybe two?

A tool imagery for Weepers who are locked into perpetual grief and mourning is an hourglass. I realize that an hourglass is not a real tool, like a powerful electric radial arm saw. However, small hourglasses have graced the stove tops of cooks forever before digital timers were built into stoves. I still have one which is well suited for boiling eggs. One easy flip and you'll know by the passing of the sand through this tiny timer tool when your eggs are boiled. It's not a macho tool, but still a tool.

It's apparent how this hourglass tool can help you with your grief vacation. I'm not suggesting you procure an hourglass that is large enough to measure a full hour or two of your potential grief vacations. But you may be able to dig through the back of your kitchen junk drawer and find a three-inch tall version. If you're so lucky to have one, park it somewhere you look every day to remind you that, while your grief continues, you can attempt to take a short vacation from it now and then.

Your grief vacation will never remove your sadness. But having a bit of space apart from your grief may help you not be owned by it. If you take an hour off from it, you haven't forgotten about your loved one. Your loved one will always be part of you.

Here's a chance to help other Weepers.

What advice do you have for Craig?

How about Jermaine?

What would you tell him?

Are You a Weeper?

Yes_____No_____ Maybe_____

If you answered yes or maybe to the above, what actions imply that you may be or have been a
Weeper?

Grief is not permanent. While our sadness over loss may linger forever, I've seen the intensity of that change over time. Since many men like to quantify and measure stuff, the tool below can help you measure how you are feeling "today" as you deal with your loss. It can help you to know if your Weeper tendencies, if you have any, are static or changing. Consider coming back to this page in 3, 6 and 12 months for reflection. If you agree to do this, put reminders on your phone or calendar now.

Yes. Right. Now.

My Weeper thoughts 3 months from my original reading of this chapter Month___Year___

My Weeper thoughts 6 months from my original reading of this chapter Month___Year___

My Weeper thoughts 12months from my original reading of this chapter Month___Year___

Peace be with all Weepers!

Chapter 4

Sheepers

"I don't know what to do!"

Lenny:

"Ugh! What now? Jasmine handled the household stuff. All I had to do was mow the yard, take care of the cars and earn my income. I don't know how to pay the bills, run the house, keep the kids' schedules, do shopping or laundry. I don't know how to find an address list to thank all the people who were so nice to us during and after the funeral.

"That woman ran everything and ran it so well... I can't believe I didn't appreciate her more for what she did. I didn't know how good I had it and I wish I could tell her that. I'm swamped, confused and overwhelmed. I just can't deal with all of this!

"But our toddler needs a bath and the older ones need back-to-school supplies. I wish I would have helped more so I know what to do! I'd do everything differently if I had another chance. I DESERVE another chance! No healthy 40-year-old woman should die suddenly like that. What's next for us? What's next for me?

"Everyone always says, "Let me know if there is anything I can do." Or, "Just call if I can help with anything." I just wish they'd simply drop by with a meal instead of me trying to figure out how to answer that question all the time. So many people have made so many offers I can't keep track of it all. It blurs together. God help us. God help me!"

Maurice:

"God, I've tried to live like a good Christian father and husband. We go to church all the time. I do good things for other people through programs there and I'm working to raise my family in the faith. Why did you take little Sarah from us? My 7-year-old didn't deserve leukemia! That was an awful death for that innocent, precious child! Why did you do that, God? Why didn't you stop it? You supposedly have the power to perform miracles!

"Why didn't you take me instead? I'm expendable. I have life insurance and my wife could have carried on and given all of our kids a life even without me. My diabetes isn't getting any better and I'm not half as good a parent as their mother is. You should have taken me! My wife deserves all 3 of her children, not just 2! Why God? Why? Why? Why? I can't get out of bed... why even try? I give up."

* * *

"What's it going to take to put you into this car today?"

Most of us have bought a new or used car along the way. Before the emerging use of the Internet to handle some of those purchase processes, we'd go to a car dealer, test drive a car and sit down at a wobbly table with a sales rep who had marginal people skills to chat about price.

Let the negotiations begin! I'd make my offer based on what I thought the market worth of the car was. Or based on what I could pay. The sales rep would scoff and go to see what he could do with his sales manager at a far-off, elevated desk. I always wondered why that desk was elevated above floor level. Perhaps to add authority and make it like a judge's bench or something? Marginally intimidating. Or at least they hoped it was, I believe.

After chatting with his sales manager, the sales rep would return with a tightened brow and demand a better offer, of course. Even if there were several back-and-forth trips, and I eventually ended up with what might be close to an OK price, I still felt violated. Hence the used car salesman stereotype. For the record, I WAS a used car salesman for a short time long ago. I wasn't very good at it and didn't like it.

Such is the case with death. We're not very good at dealing with death since it is not an everyday occurrence in our lives. We don't like it. It causes machinations in our psyche. It is a messy state of affairs and throws a monkey wrench into our whole world. We feel violated. All of our thoughts, routines, past stories, future stories, hopes and dreams are tossed to the wind. It feels like someone at an elevated desk is in control and we are not.

No wonder we want a restart. A redo. A do over. No wonder we try to make a deal with God. Even though we know deep down that the time for changing our situation has passed. And it is well beyond our control, elevated desk or not.

No wonder Maurice is pleading with God for a second chance. No wonder Lenny is sheepish about how to go on with life and has regrets about how life unfolded. No wonder that I would sometimes ask myself what I should have done differently to keep my wife and my daughter alive longer or how I could have improved the quality of their lives. Often wondering what I had to do in order to execute those "deals."

This type of mental negotiation or sheepish stagnation is real. It occurs, I believe, as a way to defer things. Inaction is a form of procrastinating about our feelings. Of avoiding the truth. A place to park or hide until things clear up.

Inaction from paralysis and after-the-fact negotiations with God can also be defense or deferment mechanisms. We think, "If I can just stay in bed," or "Maybe I can buy some time or reverse things somehow if I can change "xyz," this, then somehow everything will be different!" Of course it won't be.

Here's a related note regarding Sheepers: Many of us serve as caregivers for years before the death of our loved ones. Some people have or had slow, chronic, debilitating conditions and caregivers work for scores of months or for several years leading up to death. Guys, remember that your grief journey may start *before* the death of your loved one.

We can feel perpetual helplessness and may bargain constantly about how to change things. When we are overwhelmed by the seemingly thousands of details of caregiving, we sometimes do turn to negotiating in our heads. Sometimes this is to buy time. Other times, it may just be because we don't know what else to do. Diversion and denial, I suspect.

Jim Rohn, the now-deceased motivational speaker offered this tidbit which might help Sheepers (and others) remember that we can always get stronger: "Don't wish it were easier. Wish you were better." Mourning men know it doesn't get easier. Maybe we have to get better.

* * *

But don't tell a Sheeper that negotiating is futile. They don't want to hear about the futility of inaction or bargaining as a way to change things. I'd do whatever it took to change the outcomes. This anonymous quote may be helpful to Sheepers who are paralyzed with inaction:

> *"No amount of guilt will change the past and no amount of anxiety will change the future."*

There were many times after our family's funerals when I would just sit. I wouldn't read. I wouldn't watch TV or listen to things. I'd just sit. For hours. I wasn't negotiating. I was avoiding a few things perhaps, but it just felt right to sit alone. Yes, it was within view of dozens of pictures of my lost loved ones.

Was I being a Sheeper and overwhelmed because I didn't jump all over the many tasks that needed to be done following the funerals? I still didn't know what to do sometimes. Or I refused to do those tasks that I was well aware I needed to do. It just felt right to sit. That was different from how I have ever acted before in my life.

Being overwhelmed can give us sheep-like tendencies. Handel's *Messiah* classical musical masterpiece mentions Isaiah 53:6 which reads, "We all, like sheep, have gone astray, each of us has turned to his own way." We can become like wandering sheep when it comes to death.

We bleat or cry out. We wander, look for new grass or water or we just feel like running for no reason. Like some sheep, we may, in our grief, not even know what we want or need. Why do we turn into Sheepers? Because those bargains and wishful-thinking episodes can generate paralysis that serves up more avoidance of our painful grief. Sheepishness can be yet another device or way to defer the pain of death. The Good Shepherd can inspire us and guide us, however. What does your Good Shepherd look like? A wandering sheep gets hemmed in by shepherds, fences or that mean sheepdog. Mourning men who are Sheepers can go astray but we often get herded back by a good friend or relative who acts as our shepherd.

Your version of a Good Shepherd will lead you. For millions of men the Good Shepherd is God. Perhaps that manifests in the form of a friend or stranger who appears as needed. A "Jesus with skin on" as the saying goes. Just know that you won't be astray forever and that your Good Shepherd is imminent.

According to my friend, Thomas Kjos-Kendall, a leading Gestalt therapist from Norway, we should trust that we have inside of us what we need to heal. Trust that you'll get there on your timeline and with the resources we have inside, and with the help of our Good Shepherds.

✳✳✳

Tool imagery for a Sheeper could be a crowbar. Crowbars (also called pry bars) are rigid iron rods with narrow ends that wedge in between two things that need to be pulled apart. The narrow flat end is inserted or even pounded between the boards or items that need to be separated. The operator then pulls on or pounds on the crowbar to provide the leverage needed to pry the fixed items away from each other. These bars come in all sizes for all types of pry jobs. The visual of a crowbar can help us to examine if we are trying to leverage God. Or, it may help us ponder if we need to pry or pull ourselves apart from paralyzing inaction.

An exercise with this tool imagery is to carry around a popsicle stick in your pocket. That flimsy stick is not going to pry anything apart. But it is long and flat and can serve as a cue or a reminder about leverage. It can help us recall the benefits of not trying to leverage or bargain with God. It can also help us remember to pry ourselves apart from unhealthy paralysis or being stuck in our grief. Touching that popsicle stick when you reach into your pocket for your keys may just become a helpful, gentle nudge.

✳✳✳

Here's a chance to help a Sheeper

My Sheeper thoughts 3 months from my original
reading of this chapter Month____Year____

My Sheeper thoughts 6 months from my original
reading of this chapter Month____Year____

My Sheeper thoughts 12 months from my original
reading of this chapter Month____Year____

Peace to all Sheepers!

Chapter 5

Leapers

"Who's Next?"

Juan:

"Damn her! We were just getting our family in order and operating smoothly, and she checks out on us. Our son is headed to college in the fall and all of his over-involved activities are finally coming to an end. It's been all about him for most of his life.

"I was looking forward to some alone time with Lucia for once. We went to soooo many soccer games, choir concerts, wrestling matches, track meets, school events, church youth group trips, debate contests and fundraisers. I was exhausted after working so hard all day—it felt like I had a 2nd full-time job with all his stuff. I'm glad Lucia coordinated all that and I just had to show up.

"But she should have known about her heart. Her mother has a stent and has taken heart meds for years. So why didn't Lucia take this more seriously? I tried every trick I could to get her to pay better attention to her health and go for physicals and to take better care of herself overall. But she always said she was too busy for that and put off doctor visits, saying that she felt fine. Well nowadays, "fine" looks like a grave with her name on it over at Forest Lawn Cemetery.

"Damn it!

"I was working remotely and that would have allowed us to do some cool travel after Leonardo started college. Our priest says Lucia's sudden death is going to make me mourn for a long time. But she's been in the ground for a month now and the boy is off to college soon. So, I'm all alone. I'm wondering how this online dating thing works. My wife of 20 years isn't here for me now, so who will be?"

Lee:
"I think of Suzie every day. I'm still sad but I'm also so disappointed. Who could have predicted her having that tragic death? It just changes everything. I'm now a solo dad to two elementary-aged kids who miss their mommy a lot. Suzie and I shared the household duties so I know what's going on around here but I don't want to do it all by myself. I'm not sure if I can!

"These kids are in so many sports and activities— I'm not sure I can handle all that alone. Especially with the high demands of my work. Suzie pushed me to earn and accept that promotion but she never appreciated the demands of the new role. I don't have energy for everything. Something's gotta give! Why did she have to leave us? Especially with no warning!

"I know I shouldn't be mad at her but that's how I feel. Abandoned, alone, lonely, overworked, and overwhelmed. Not what I pictured age 40 to look like! I'm going to have to tell the kids that they'll have to give up some things now that there is less time and money to go around since we lost Suzie's income.

"Annabelle from our church is divorced, attractive and has no kids. She seems to have it together and would be a good companion, I think. She'd be very helpful to our household, if she's open to a relationship. Even though she knew I was married, she seemed a little flirty to me that one time at the church's adult group hayrack ride. I wonder how soon is "too soon" to approach her?"

* * *

"Look Before You Leap!" That phrase has been uttered by advice givers since whenever advice was first given. This Type of Male Mourning is a "Leaper." A leap is a jump. A Leaper Type is a man who jumps too fast into his next relationship, buzz, deal, career change, relocation or major decision. A Leaper Type may be a man who:

- Gets married or falls into a new romantic relationship just weeks or months after the death of his spouse.
- Sells the family house where he and his wife lived for years "just to make a change" or to "get away from the memories."
- Up and quits his job shortly after his son or daughter dies because he is "a mess."
- Two months after his loss, ends all his past social relationships or church connections so that he and his new girlfriend can travel the world.

Some men like Juan and Lee get or stay angry for a time after the death of a loved one. And they act quickly driven by anger, insecurity, fear, a need for approval or simply denial of the death. Or they withdraw or bargain.

Many sources say that anger is the result of feeling trapped, in danger, overly vulnerable or being treated unfairly. Dr. Lisa Shulman talks about how grief is "traumatic" and provokes a fight or flight response to the brain.

Her book on the topic is *Before and After Loss: A Neurologist's Perspective on Loss, Grief and Our Brain.* She says grief can make us feel like we are in danger. I agree that grief feels like trauma. Anger can be the normal, logical reaction to that trauma.

Few can say that there is or was no trauma-induced anger surrounding the loss of their beloved. I have heard several "peaceful departure" stories and I know that not everyone left behind is mad. Most are sad, but many death stories come and go peacefully without anger. However, death of our loved ones can leave us feeling like we are in danger, overly vulnerable or cheated.

Death of our loved ones then is a perfect recipe for anger. A recipe that serves up fight- or flight-related trauma. However, anger, in some cases, protects us. Anger-fueled adrenalin can mean a faster getaway from a threat. It can mean more strength for our blows if we have to defend ourselves from an attacker. It can allow us to survive.

So how about the anger of Juan and Lee? Are there saber-tooth tigers chasing after them? Not likely. Should they *not* be angry then after death? They are safe and physically secure, most likely, so why the rage and urge to act suddenly? The answer to that is above: trauma. We are simply feeling trauma. Massive change leads to massive emotions.

Since anger about death is normal, then isn't it OK for us to Leap? Isn't it OK to look for another wife, drink, drug, sexual episode, adrenalin fix, crazy job or some other type of diversion?

Shouldn't it be OK to cloak, mask, reduce or delete that pain and anger?

Experts say there's no one right way to grieve or mourn and no proper, neat pathway for it. So, who am I to say that Juan and Lee, who may still be in an angry, grief-induced daze, are wrong? Their reactions may be normal, but are they too quick? Are they using their leap as a way to cover up hurt or anger?

This isn't about how long a man *should* wait to remarry, if ever. It is more about tracking stuff. About knowing where you are. It is helpful for us to know what's fueling our decisions about our next leap. What's driving us to make a (hasty) move? What if we wait a few weeks, months or years to make a more informed, not-as-emotional decision? How immediate should or shouldn't our leaps be? Asking and answering these questions on a repeated basis is a healthy exercise.

The opposite extreme to Juan and Lee are guys who become hermits. They shut themselves off from the world for too long—however long *too long* is. Perhaps they never take down their shrines to the departed. They stay in Sweeper or Sheeper mode for a long time. They still refer to everything as "our, ours, we and us" even years after their wife has died. Perhaps they develop unhealthy lifestyle habits. Perhaps they will never consider remarriage due to the pain they've been through. They don't ever want to consider getting that close to someone ever again.

Those choices are fine since we all grieve differently. The fact that someone else's decisions are different than the ones we'd make still doesn't mean that they deserve our negative judgment. Live and let live (unless someone is a danger to himself) I suggest.

When should guys leap?

Obviously, this is about balance. There are no rules about when to sell the house, get a girlfriend, give away your daughter's clothes, change jobs, change churches, change cities, switch friends, change companions, swap out our diet, quit or start drinking heavily. But there should be a rule about the need for balance. Are your decisions being weighed carefully?

Anger, fear, trauma, vulnerability, or the feeling of being cheated all form that perfect storm or foundation for moves that may be too fast or unhealthy. Or, conversely, too slow of a decision or action. Most guys figure it out. I throw out this dipstick so we can all check our emotional oil at this moment in time, if in fact we are about to do some crazy leaps.

Is your anger or denial crankcase half empty or half full? Does it need to be topped off? Or totally changed? Is your engine close to blowing due to a dry crankcase? Are you managing it all? Emotions are not machines but they do need tracking, awareness and ongoing maintenance.

But some men are not meant to be alone.

Here's the true story of one transparent Leaper: A woman shared that her mother had died. She then told me about her father, who was in his sixties at the time. Her father remarried within three months of his wife's death. The daughter told me, "He had to get remarried quickly because he is a horny old dude!" As I said, all relationships and decisions are unique!

Some men just don't operate well as a single entity. They may have run a business or had a highly responsible job but they always relied on their spouse to run the household. They may feel like they need a spouse/partner to help them do that even after the death of their loved one(s). Or they simply need someone else in their lives from a companionship standpoint.

That's OK and normal for their grief and life journeys. Self-awareness on this front is priceless.

If you meet an available partner who is interested in you, why not start a relationship? I know of a man who nurtured his wife through cancer for three years and, after she was gone, he became unofficially engaged in just a few months. They eventually married and were together for 20 years before death separated them. They knew each other socially before both of their spouses died, so this was a very logical and correct-feeling story. Only winners there. What's your story? What do you want it to look like? What will you make it look like?

Lee above asks, "How soon is too soon?" That answer is unique to each individual and couple, so there are no formula answers. Successful relationships are complex and need to be thoroughly discussed. The elephant in the room is that the dead spouse will always be part of any widower's life and new couples need to be aware of that.

Some men feel it is God's plan that they came together with another partner quickly. It probably is—who can say that is wrong? Sometimes that happens too quickly for your adult offspring, whose dead mother is irreplaceable in their eyes. If you move on too fast in their eyes, the kids may feel their mother's memory is being dishonored and they may be angry with you.

They may think you are doing something wrong. They have a lot invested in the life of their mother so they are naturally emotional and grieving in their own ways. Our role as grieving men is to listen to your kids and hear their stories of mourning. Here's an important thing to remember: their journeys are not like yours.

Your adult kids are a generation younger than you. They may be living outside of your world (a different apartment / house / city, etc.). They may not live alone like you. If they have their own kids, their own jobs or their own college lives or whatever, they don't come home to the same empty house that you do.

You are the one living alone now. You are the one whose social routine has likely changed. You are the one who yells at the empty house about the unfairness of it all. Maybe you're retired and now you don't even have a job to go to and now you don't have a spouse. Only that lonely house which is hard to adjust to. Your adult offspring likely don't have that same dilemma.

What's the bottom line on this? If you hear from your kids or other relatives something to the effect that you are moving forward too soon, don't be angry with them. You can be the family leader and hero for recognizing this and addressing it. Be sure to hear what they are saying but just love them. In most cases, their opinions are coming from a helpful heart.

* * *

A different side of the same coin is the dating scene for widowers. An expert in the grief support field reminded me that sometimes the adult children of a fresh widower have good reason to be concerned about someone new in the widower's life. The kids may see the forest when your spouse dies but you're only seeing the trees. Their concerns can be well-founded in some cases, because scammers are out there.

Most new love connections are positive and innocent, but a grieving man can be a target as well. It is easier than ever to find out information about men in transition. Think about it guys; obituaries are public and online so the whole world can figure out who has just lost a wife. Most mortuaries post the dead person's life story online which describes family members. Even if the local newspaper is not where the obituary is listed, the mortuary usually does make a public death announcement.

If you've been married for decades, you most likely don't think in these terms so I'll speak bluntly. A scamming woman can very easily learn who is now single and those new singles are almost always an emotional mess. They often are seeking comfort. Widowers also must remember that it's relatively easy for an outsider to deduce who may have assets.

From your family's obituary, a scammer can often learn the church you belong to if a funeral was held there. In many cases you likely live in a zip code somewhere around that church. Your zip code can often be an indicator of income levels. Older guys' home addresses are typically available in phone books in libraries or available in online search tools for pennies or even for free.

Have you placed your employer and job title on social media? Millions of men do. From that, scammers can easily figure out where you work and at what level. Especially attractive to a scammer would be a widower who owns a business.

Hopefully this kind of thing is an exception but be sure to avoid *being* that exception. Just remember that men in mourning have heads full of mush. Men with assets should be especially aware if someone new just pops into their life. Or, sometimes a woman with bad motives can emerge from the ranks of people you already know.

A good way to safeguard yourself is to talk with other guys who have been through the death of their spouse. Talk with guys who have remarried, guys who have not and even guys who will never remarry. They will have a more objective viewpoint than you might. Find these male sounding boards through your friendship base, your mortuary's staff, your church or a grief group. Don't trust someone you meet in a social media chat group. That's a great place for a scammer to hang out. Remember that you are driven more by emotions these days than you ever have been in your life.

Also know that scammers and gold-diggers can be of both genders. New widows are also highly emotional and can easily be targets of men who use the strategies mentioned. Everyone needs to look before they leap.

* * *

Some men meet their new "next" through friends, church, neighbors, workplaces, relatives, randomly, a bar, online—several different ways. Maybe even through a grief support group.

The way folks come together is not important. Although one needs to use extra caution if they were to find their next soulmate online somewhere. What's important is that couples know what they are getting into. As a widower, are you truly ready for a new relationship? Really? Or are you simply masking your pain with this new "leap?"

As a chronic observer of people, I submit that all parties in the remarriage or re-partnering equation check their emotional dipsticks. Guys are often quantitative, so remember to learn about and check your new partner's emotions as well as your own.

I've fallen in love before. With my wife and my newborn kids. It is an overwhelmingly giddy feeling. Getting to know someone new who has an interest in us gives us a dopamine rush. Dopamine, a neurotransmitter in the brain, plays a big part in how we feel pleasure, according to webmd.com. What widower doesn't want to feel pleasure again? "Where is my Next?" we ask.

Remember that grief can be buried, denied, diverted, bargained with and more. There is a lot to process. And if we leap quickly before we are ready, that grief can still come out later in some form, somehow, sometime. Have you "processed" your grief? Are you sure it isn't going to jump up inside of your new relationship? Is that fair to your new partner if it does? Have you two talked about it? More than once?

I'm aware of a widower who was not looking for a new relationship. But you've heard about those well-meaning friends who are always trying to set someone up with a date. Well, his friends insisted on introducing him to a long-divorced woman they knew.

The couple instantly clicked and were married in less than a year after the widower's wife died. They communicated about "the other woman" in the widower's life and they seem like instant soulmates. The parents-in-law of the widower told the man that he and their daughter had enjoyed a great life. They told him they knew that he has a great capacity for love and that he should go on and love another. What an amazing, mature and wonderful outlook. More power to them all!

Since there are more than seven billion people living on Earth, I personally believe there can be more than one soulmate here for you. The odds are pretty good that there is someone else out there who is a fit for you. Especially if you're looking for that.

Remember though, a new partner will not be your "first." Your Next is at least your second (or third?) love, so I suspect your emotional journey together will be different. You have experienced a myriad of firsts with your now-dead wife. This history cannot be repeated with someone else. I suggest mourning men need to set proper self-expectations, as well as expectations as a couple within their future relationships.

A tool imagery for Leapers is a level. A level is a three-dimensional, ruler-like device which stands on its edge. It often has inch and centimeter marks on it, with a hole in the middle that is fitted with a small vial containing a greenish liquid with a bubble inside.

The purpose of a level is to tell you that some surface is on the level. If you're repairing your wooden deck in the back yard and putting up railings, you'll want to hold the level on both the horizontal and vertical boards to ensure they are, in fact, level and straight. This is key before you nail or screw them in place. When the level is held against a horizontal surface and the bubble is in the middle of the vial, the surface is "level." When the level is held against a vertical surface and the bubble is in the middle, it's "plumb." In order to build a stable, functional structure, leveling is critical.

The level is an essential tool in carpentry or cement projects. The bubble tells the truth about your project. You may have put hours of emotional, even skilled work into your project and think you are home-free. But when the pesky bubble doesn't align inside the lines, you know there's more work to do.

There's a level for every type of project or job you are working on. They can quantify or measure most anything.

If you are concerned that you may be leaping before you look or jumping into something too soon in your grief, consider the level. Picture yourself holding a level against your chest. Of course, your curved body will never allow the bubble to fit between its lines of perfection, but you get the idea.

Some of your family, friends, other grieving guys or folks at your church may be saying "slow down, Lee!" Maybe we should consider listening to some of that. Maybe they see things more clearly than those of us with heads full of mush.

No, they likely can't relate to our grief and heartache and the strong desire to mask our pain. But they may well be acting as levels in our lives. Maybe they are that little green bubble trying to keep us straight and plumb. Maybe they're helping us to avoid nailing or screwing that beam in place because they can see that it's crooked, tilted, or dysfunctional. Maybe they know that the "project" we're working on still needs tweaking.

Most hardware stores carry levels that are pocket size. Keeping one of those in our pockets might be wise if folks are telling us that we are displaying Leaper-like tendencies.

So, Leapers can be all over the map. Some men leap before they look. Most don't, but this is not a normal time in a man's life. The bottom line is that men who have lost loved ones to death need to level things out and quantify our emotions and the big picture amidst life-changing decisions. Just like everyone else.

***

Here's a chance to help a Leaper

What guidance do you have for Juan?

How about Lee? What would you tell him?

Are you a Leaper?

Yes_____ No_____ Maybe_____

If you answered yes or maybe to the above, what actions imply that you may be or have been a
Leaper?

Grief is not permanent. While our sadness over loss may linger forever, I've seen the intensity of that change over time. Since many men like to quantify and measure stuff, the tool below can help you measure how you are feeling "today" as you deal with your loss. It can help you to know if your Leaper tendencies, if you have any, are static or changing. Consider coming back to this page in 3, 6 and 12 months for reflection. If you agree to do this, put reminders on your phone or calendar now.

Yes. Right. Now.

My Leaper thoughts 3 months from my original reading of this chapter Month___Year__

My Leaper thoughts 6 months from my original reading of this chapter Month___Year__

My Leaper thoughts 12 months from my original reading of this chapter Month___Year__

Peace to all Leapers!

Chapter 6

Keepers

"I'm Still Here"

Mike:

"Wendy's terminal illness was awful. I took care of her for four years at home but eventually her doctor said she'd gotten beyond my ability to care for her. I couldn't do the IVs and catheters and her long list of what seemed like hourly medications. The daily parade of clinical people who came to the house became too much to manage, especially since I still had my job. I hated moving her into that rehab place but there was no choice. Even Wendy thought it would be better.

"I was thrilled when I was allowed to do my job remotely four days a week so I could be with her. I knew all the staffers there at the facility, their menu rotations, and the activities schedule. Heck I even knew the TV channel guide by heart. It was like we were both residents there. But they couldn't stop her decline.

"Wendy knew she was going to die and I really didn't want to believe it. I still don't. The good thing is that we could plan together. There's nothing worse than planning a funeral with a living person who's been your partner for over 30 years. You'd think it would be peaceful and collaborative but it just made everything too real and sad. But that process kind of gave me peace since it made for less decision making when the overwhelming end came.

"It is all still raw. I've tried shutting myself off from others, being angry at God for taking her, and I've even had a few too many drinks in my too-quiet home. None of that helps; she's still gone. I went to a professional counselor 5 five months after Wendy's death. He was helpful when he said, "*You didn't die,*" when I was moaning about loneliness. Those were three important words.

"He also encouraged me to fret less about not thinking about her all the time by reminding me that I didn't think about her 24/7 when she was *alive.* Since her body was so ravaged by illness and we have a strong faith, I feel she's in a much better place now. I'm sure of it.

"So, I suppose I need to heed the counselor's advice and not stay in this funk forever. I'm still here and there are still things I can do for the rest of my family. But I don't want to do them alone. We were always supposed to do those things together! She'll always be the most important part of me, but at least she's at peace now. Those two thoughts will carry me forward. But damn, I miss her!"

Terrence:

"I know I'm supposed to forgive that guy who ran the red light, but I'm nowhere close to that yet. Even though it has been 11 months since the funeral I still can't make sense out of all of this.

Natalie was going places in her career and our youngest now has his own place. Things were shaping up to be a really nice time in our lives.

"But now look at me! I'm a mess. After the crash I asked God to change it and told Him that I should have been the one to go instead of beautiful Natalie. But of course, that's a futile conversation. So, then I just pretended nothing happened and tried to bury things. I showed up back to work more quickly than people thought I should. I avoided painful conversations with all the well-meaning morons. But that didn't get me anywhere either because I was still sad—and somewhat mad all the time.

"We just celebrated Christmas. The kids all came home and decorated everything just like Natalie used to. I couldn't have done that. We ate the traditional foods that we always do. We decided to skip gift-giving since that's supposed to be all joyful and such. Nobody thought stuff would bring us joy this year. But then a joyful thing did happen. The kids sat around and talked about their mother. I cried a ton. You'd think I cried because I missed not having her here. But that wasn't it. I didn't cry because she was gone. I cried because she was *there*.

"My wife lives in each of our four kids. She lives on differently in each kid. I can see her humor, her looks, her movements, her style of speaking, her personality, her politics and her faith sprinkled heavily throughout all of our kids. I still get pangs of hurt and loss randomly all the time. For months I said to myself, "I can't wait to tell Wendy about this!" And then the sadness hit me again when in an instant I realized that I couldn't do that. But daily chats with my kids and grandkids on the smartphone are such a blessing since I get to see her "in" the kids and grandkids that way. But I wish she was here!"

* * *

Keepers are just that: keepers of the good stuff. As author and grief counselor Sharon Zehndar explains, "We need to decide what memories we are going to hold on to and which memories we are going to let go." I agree and contend that Keepers have figured out how to let go of the bad stuff and hold on to the good memories. Here are some characteristics of Keepers:

- ✓ They keep trying to make sense or find meaning in their losses or tragedies.
- ✓ They work to NOT blame God for the death(s) of their beloved(s).
- ✓ They strive to forgive the person who caused their loved one's death, if there is one.
- ✓ They slowly start disposing of the deceased's belongings, keeping several special items.
- ✓ They do their best to stay busy in order to avoid sadness in a too-quiet house. They reflect on their actions to ascertain if they are masking their grief.
- ✓ They proactively ask family and friends to get together even after the invitations stop.
- ✓ They maintain their worship routines, devotionals, and study their holy books for guidance.
- ✓ They maintain their commitment to their surviving family/kids even though it is hard doing that alone.

✓ They keep a special place for items in their homes to visually remind them of their departed.

✓ They acknowledge that they're still here so they try to exercise and eat right even though meals are now different.

✓ They understand that their kids' grief journey is different than their own.

✓ They take comfort knowing that young kids are resilient and have abundant faith and optimism.

✓ They realize that grief heals layer by layer, like a broken bone.

✓ They know that it took years to build their old life and their new life will also take time to rebuild.

✓ They avoid "If I had only…" statements.

✓ They sense that unresolved issues with their loved ones may be different than grief, and they remain open to seeking professional help.

✓ They keep looking at old pictures until they become a source of happiness and gratitude for time together versus sadness.

✓ They still have faith even when God doesn't appear to give us answers to our questions.

✓ They remember that separate death events each require their own grief journey.

✓ They recognize that death is not the only cause of grief in life.

✓ They stay in touch with a grief buddy or buddies— people who understand loss. They understand that grief and pain don't go away—that they just get used to it. They don't feel guilty when they find their smile again.

Whew! That's quite a list!

Most of us won't get through this whole list in a lifetime. The list is simply a framework or backdrop for grief healing. "You don't get over it, you just get used to it," is attributed to Carlene Vester Eneroth in her book, "Does Anyone Else Hurt This Bad and Live?" That is a heavy title but her quote is profound. Our new life trajectory is forever different.

* * *

Becoming a Keeper does not mean conquering the long list above. It is more like *living* that list rather than *conquering* it. Keepers can simplify things by boiling it down to this shorter list:

- ✓ We'll keep our lost loved ones in our hearts and minds.
- ✓ We'll keep working to forgive ourselves and others, if needed. We'll keep mindful that we are still here for a reason.

While more manageable, even this shorter list is a tall order. Becoming a Keeper is a lifelong endeavor. Have you started on that journey?

* * *

Tool imagery for a Keeper is varnish. Yes, varnish. "That's not a tool," you argue, and you're right, of course. A saw cuts wood. A router trims it. A sander smooths it.

"Those are real tools, Paul."

I agree. Varnish is what you use when all of those tasks are completed. You apply varnish when your part or piece is in place—or about to be put in place. In some ways, it is just as important as all of those other tools because of what it adds to the finished product.

Consider the lowly magazine rack I created in high school shop class all those years ago. I drew, measured, cut, screwed, leveled, glued and sanded the pieces all into a (rickety) final product. It was not a thing of beauty, but you could tell it was a magazine rack. Its padded, flip-up lid served as a footrest.

Before the padding and vinyl were added to the flip up door on top, the final step was to varnish it. I sanded some more and added the perfect color of varnish to the finished product. The color actually matched a couple of pieces of furniture we had at home. The pride in my work grew as I added color to it and watched the varnish soak into the virgin wood and *change it forever*. I fixed the globs and bubbles, and smoothed it all on with love.

The end result was a transformed product. Its less-than-perfect measurements assured that it was still rickety, however the look improved immensely. The plain, whitish pine had been transformed into a warm, inviting Early American-looking piece. The varnish was not a tool, but it was a final change agent and the finishing touch to what the other tools helped to create.

Next time you see an item of furniture with a pleasing color, keep in mind that varnish did that. It changed a raw, bare, (beat up?) piece of furniture from one thing into something else more beautiful.

Pick out a beautifully-colored furniture item you see all the time. It can be the same one you chose for the assignment about sanding. As you see or touch that item each day, know that your Keeper mindset is like varnish —it makes the end product functional and, eventually, beautiful. Beautiful, I hope, like your memories of your loved one.

Keeper Reflections:

How would you respond to Mike?

What thoughts do you have for Terrence?

Are YOU a Keeper?

Yes_____No_____Maybe_____

If you answered yes or maybe to the above, what actions imply that you may be a **Keeper**?

Grief is not permanent. While our sadness over loss may linger forever, I've seen the intensity of that change over time. Since many men like to quantify and measure stuff, the tool below can help you measure how you are feeling "today" as you deal with your loss. It can help you to know if your Keeper tendencies—if you have any—are static or changing. Consider coming back to this page in 3, 6 and 12 months for reflection. If you agree to do this, put reminders on your phone or calendar now.

Yes. Right. Now!

My Keeper thoughts 3 months from my original reading of this chapter Month___Year___

My Keeper thoughts 6 months from my original reading of this chapter Month___Year___

My Keeper thoughts 12 months from my original reading of this chapter Month___Year___

Peace to all Keepers!

Chapter 7

How Many TEARS Today?

Some men cry at their losses. Some men don't. But I suggest that all men have TEARS. I'm not talking about the moisture that runs out of your eyes and down your face. Oh, those tears are real and usually present themselves around death stories, memories and loss.

A TEARS Moment

Here's another way of looking at tears: Use TEARS as an acronym to address—or at least recognize—those hourly, daily, and weekly mini-grief episodes we experience so often after the loss of our loved one(s). Most everyone in mourning experiences these moments, I believe.

You know what I'm talking about if you ever say to yourself, "Oh, we used to love going to that restaurant," "Oh, that's the orthopedic clinic we went to so many times," or, that hospital, or that doctor's office or that specialist or that store or *this* store or that other store or that theater or this church or that friend's house or that park, etc.

In my experience, a simple drive through town became a nagging nightmare of memory lane. It was almost too painful to go anywhere. Because we lived in our city for such a long period of time, we had many, many memories associated with specific places. The distraction was so great that I'd sometimes forget where I was headed!

And there is the constant cycling in our heads at home, at church and virtually everywhere. "Remember when Lisa wore this sweater all the time at Christmas?" Or, "Where did Laura ever get that really ugly Christmas sweater for her workplace Ugly Sweater Contest anyway?" Even something as simple as the bowl your wife used for cereal can cause a reaction in you. You and I have thousands of these examples.

I just had a new flash the other day when I drove past a company that sells bricks for new home construction. Lisa and I excitedly walked through their rows of brick façade inventory more than *35 years ago*. I've driven past that place several times since her death, yet that night, the brick-picking memory hit me hard, out of the blue. The original event occurred decades ago, yet there I was, flashing back and tearing up like it was yesterday. If you're a griever, you get this. I call these mini-grief memories "T.E.A.R.S. Moments."

T is for Trigger

Any grieving person has triggers—even men. We get triggered by anything and everything related to our departed loved one. We all have hundreds of people, places and things that kick off an instant memory related to our lost loved ones.

Those triggers come 24/7 at first (yes, even in our dreams). We can't stop thinking about the departed. Funeral week doesn't help since you have to rehash the lost loved one's entire life by writing an obituary, contributing funeral sermon anecdotes, picking out favorite hymns, compiling photos and memorabilia for the obligatory picture bulletin boards and bling table. And perhaps the hardest: choosing the music and the pictures for the video version of their lives.

Then there's the coordination with family and friends regarding travel and so on. It is a lot. Triggers everywhere!

Then the funeral week is over. People go home and back to work. The casseroles slow down and eventually stop coming. Things get quieter. If you can, you go back to work or your normal daily routine. But the triggers keep coming. Maybe even now more often than ever. Am I going crazy? Will I ever be able to think of anything else? That's normal. If you don't have any triggers of memories, you should consider rereading the Sweeper chapter.

E is for Emotion

Triggers and emotion go hand in hand. The trigger is the person, place or thing that reminds you of what you experienced with your loved one. Then you immediately react *emotionally* to that trigger.

For me it is often a subtle, almost unconscious gasp, followed by a hint of a moist eye. This poke is short-lived. Most of them are painful because they are typically about good memories and the realization you won't be going to that restaurant, communion service, theater or Walgreen's together ever again. Some triggered emotions are more intense than others. Even driving by "that place" a second or third or tenth time doesn't necessarily diminish that emotional impact.

Some triggers don't cause tons of emotion, but many do. The triggers' accompanying emotions can be ongoing. And new ones keep appearing. Holidays or rare visits or other "first-time-without-them" events, for example. The first Valentine's Day without my wife seemed especially hard.

A recent trip with friends to a movie theater was an after-death first for me. For the first time in the previous 18 months, I walked into the big, darkened room. My radar immediately started scoping out the handicapped seating locations. That's when my TEARS Moment hit. I didn't need to find handicapped seating anymore.

I get sad just writing about this. Going to the movies was our thing. We had it down to a science about how to scope out what was showing at "the cheap seats" (discount theater) and what times the shows would be on. We even developed a shorthand with good friends about how to meet there and at what time. For instance, a message on the *answering machine* (yes, this an old story) was something like: "Kill Bill. Cheap Seats. 7 PM." No "Hello," or "See you there?" That was the whole message. So going to a movie recently was a huge TEARS Moment for me.

A is for Adjust

If you are driving and are impacted by a trigger and its accompanying emotions, remember to be safe. The teenager driving in the lane next to you doesn't care that you're spacing out—he's too focused on his cell phone. The two of you are a potential disaster.

The need to adjust therefore is important. Since Triggers and emotions come steadily and randomly, we need to be aware of their effect. They will slide us into a funk instantly. But how long do we spend in that funk? Do we realize our state is altered? We likely need to adjust to these triggers and emotions, either consciously or subconsciously.

As I mentioned, when I asked my counselor if I was dishonoring my loved ones because I started thinking about them *less*, he suggested that I didn't think about them 100% of the time when they were living. So therefore, I was not dishonoring their memory when my frequent triggers, emotions, and adjustments didn't come 24/7 anymore. We eventually figure out that it is not healthy to obsess non-stop about our losses, I guess.

But I still have TEARS Moments, again and again. And I adjust. Even though TEARS Moments don't come constantly now, they still come and I still need to adjust often. New grievers, and I'm not going to define what "new" means, will have more TEARS Moments than folks who are farther down the path of healing. That's normal.

After Triggers, Emotion and Adjust, we reflect.

R is for Reflection

Reflection is the review of our loss. We are reminded about our loved one by the person, place or thing that triggered this replay of a specific old memory. Reflecting on those moments is bittersweet in many cases. If it is a good or great memory, we'll first be happy about that wonderful memory. But if our grief is new and raw, that sweet memory gets washed away quickly in a mental tidal wave of loss.

We realize that we'll never experience that person, place, or thing with our loved one again. That hurts. It is a huge sense of loss. Loss about what could have or would have or even should have been. Now it's not going to be realized, ever. We are forced to hover on lost potential and a lost future.

We can try to manage reflections. I've set a goal that the next time I walk into a movie theater I'm not going to be so sad about not having to find the wheelchair space for seating. Instead, I'm going to work to reflect on how much fun I had going to so many movies with my bride.

What personal reflections do you settle on after these frequent triggers and emotional moments? All couples and families have their inside jokes and fun private histories. It's what makes a couple a couple, and a family a family. Savor those reflections as they come.

S is for Sigh

You have been triggered, gotten emotional, made adjustments, and are reflecting. The TEARS acronym is completed with a *sigh*.

Not the kind of sarcastic sigh that people sometimes obnoxiously stretch out and do to tell you that they are superior to you. No, I'm talking about a good sigh. When we get done with something strenuous, tense or even a pleasurable action, we often make a good sigh. A kind of closing statement. A cleansing type of breath.

Meditation aficionados and yoga fans know about cleansing breaths and controlled deep breathing. My daughter, Laura, was into yoga and she often discussed the benefits of breathing deeply. This was almost ironic for a young lady who was dependent on external oxygen 24/7 for more than four years. She preached about good breathing and good sighs.

Laura never played the "victim" card, despite her drawing the short straw of health in her life. At age 28, she had a 23-hour-long open-heart surgery which was supposed to take four hours.

Afterwards she endured complications from being on an ICU ventilator for too long. She became mobile after months of in-patient rehab, but was tethered to external oxygen sources forever.

Other than an occasional outburst swearing at a misbehaving oxygen tank, she rarely complained about her lot in life.

She joined the public speaking group, Toastmasters, in order to build her speaking skills. She wanted to become a motivational speaker to inspire others based on her personal health journey and story. In the back of this book is a link to a video of her early motivational speaking efforts. I'm a proud Dad.

Like Laura preached, we can benefit from finishing something good with a positive, cleansing sigh. Try it right now. Think of a positive memory and then let out a big, long relaxed sigh. It can entrench your reflections more deeply.

That final, conscious action concludes a TEARS Moment. It puts a punctuation mark on the event. It summarizes it, captures and identifies it, Until the next one comes, which, of course, will happen soon.

* * *

A look at *your* TEARS Moments:

> What was your most recent positive trigger about your lost loved one?
>
>
> What emotion did you immediately feel when triggered?

How did you adjust to that emotion?

What reflections did you have about that event, person, place or thing?

Did you let out a cleansing sigh at the end?

Constant triggers and TEARS Moments can be grueling. But, again, they are normal and needed, not something to avoid. Even negative reflections have a role in our healing journeys. TEARS Moments are just another way to get a handle on our grief.

Peace to all who have TEARS Moments!

Chapter 8

How to Kill Your Elephant

Telling Your Death Story

Elephants are amazing creatures worthy of our respect and preservation efforts. The headline for this chapter is obviously hyperbole. For decades in business, I've heard the phrases, "We need to address the elephant in the room" or "don't ignore the 800-pound gorilla." They are standard jargon for Corporate America as it attempts to deal with the obvious.

Author Sharon Zehnder was the first person I've heard relate the "elephant in the room" concept to death. That was profound. How many of us widowers go back to family, church, work or social situations where our lost loved one is not even mentioned or acknowledged in any way?

How do you feel, guys, when people don't say anything about your loss? Why don't they bring it up? These are loving and helpful people but I feel they don't want to bring things up "again" because they don't want to cause us pain. They think that if they address the elephant in the room, they'll refresh our pain all over again. They think they're picking that scab and that will cause us harm. So, they don't want to bring it up. But Mourning Men are *always* thinking about it, aren't we?

Not addressing the fact that we have lost our loved one disrespects our major life transition. Not addressing the loss of our parents, sons, daughters, brothers, sisters, spouses, friends or relatives happens frequently. And it means that others are ignoring what might just be the most traumatic thing that has ever happened to us.

I heard a story about a widower I know who went to his extended family's major holiday celebration just a few months after the passing of his wife. His relatives are nice, loving people, but they simply didn't bring up the recent death of his wife! I'm told the gathering went on as if nothing unusual had even happened. They weren't being mean or cruel. I suspect that they simply didn't want to cause the widower pain by reminding him about it. However, it was more painful for *him* to have to bring up the obvious topic.

Since the deaths of my daughter and my wife, I've met, interviewed, and come to know dozens of other people who are grieving the deaths of loved ones. So far, I've found no exceptions to this rule: When I ask mourners for their stories about the deaths of their loved ones, they *want* to tell me about it. They *need* to talk about it. We need our communities to listen to us.

I can see relief when a survivor tells their story!

It makes me sad that too many grievers/mourners have not been able to tell their loved one's death stories often enough. Families don't want to ask or rehear the stories over and over. They too feel pain, and they also want to shelter us. They feel awkward about it all. Friends and coworkers don't want to pick that scab either so they also often ignore our elephants.

But most of us guys prefer that the elephant in the room be slain. We want to tell our stories. We want others to know about it and to empathize with us in our loss. It helps us remember our special people and we want you to remember them too!

* * *

An example of this is a widow I met at a grief class. She went through a multi-week course with a large group which often broke into smaller discussion groups. She is an introvert and during the small group discussion sessions she would never fight her way into the conversation. The extroverts dominated and she sat in silence most of the time.

But in a different social setting, I asked her about her loss. Not for any real reason—I just hadn't heard it. In this setting, there were no extroverts dominating the table and no time limits. We were just having a relaxed conversation.

The manner in which she told the story of her husband's rapid death told me a lot. I could tell that she was not practiced with telling the tale. It was obvious that she had not told it many times. Her adult children likely had heard it and maybe a few good friends. But she'd apparently not told many others her story.

We should be able to tell the death stories of our loved ones in a well-practiced fashion. There should be enough people in our lives who have asked us about our loved ones that we are able to cleanly and honestly communicate their death story. Why? Because this is just too much to keep bottled up inside of us.

Many grievers don't want to burden their personal networks with stories of death and dying. People in our communities assume that with the passage of time that we are OK. Especially if our stories don't come up too often. But if people around us don't want to hear what we need to tell them, perhaps we should supplement those communities with new friends, contacts or even grief groups that *will* address our needs.

Grief work takes more than just the passage of time. Most of us heal a little bit more each time we get to tell our story of our loved ones. Those who disagree with this theory should check out chapters 1 through 4 in this book.

If our departed loved ones don't come up in conversation at family holidays or other social events, it is OK for us to bring them up tactfully. We should not dominate the conversation with it or be a broken record wherever we go. When it's appropriate, it is OK for our friends and supporters to know and hear that we are still thinking about those who've died. Everyone is afraid of picking the scab, but our supporters need to know we still may want to remember and discuss our loved ones.

Our supporters should know that they can focus on life stories. They can ask us things like: "You often took trips around Christmas. Which one was her favorite trip?" Our friends don't need to be a credentialed counselor to get us talking about special and favorite experiences with our loved ones. Even something as simple as, "Remember when we went to the Fourth of July parade and your dog couldn't stop barking at the clowns?" If our friends bring up crazy memories with us, we'll feel better. Make it comfortable for them to open that door.

Chapter 9

What Your Dentist Knows About
"The Calm After the Storm"

The Calm After the Storm is just what it sounds like. In Middle America and elsewhere, friends, relatives, coworkers, church pals, neighbors and others flock toward the death storm. They show their humanity to us through food, cards, money gifts, memorials, scholarships, rides, lodging, more food, yard work, home repairs and social media testimonials. Did I mention food?

Those displays of love clearly enable us to somehow survive our shock of loss. It did for me and my family. I'm blessed to have a wonderful support infrastructure but I know people who have lost loved ones who are not so lucky. Yes, they benefit from the tsunami of support that typically shows up right after death. This wave of support is especially strong if it is a younger person who died or someone who died in a tragic or sudden death.

But how long does this support continue? How long should it continue? Every person is different, every situation is different, but there are some things mourning men will appreciate. The Calm After the Storm sees our supporters settling back into their normal routines. It appears to them or is presumed that mourning men are doing that, too. But we're not.

What does a dentist have to do with The Calm After the Storm? A lot. Dentists are masters of schedule. My physician didn't have much luck booking me for my next appointment by saying, "See you in a few months." My follow-up appointment was for something minor so I left his office with no appointment.

My dentist's office was brutal, however. At least on the appointment-setting front. Dental insurance apparently covers routine teeth cleaning every six months. Do you think my dentist's office, which has mastered aggressive strategies, was going to let me go with a hope-filled promise of seeing them in a few months? Not bloody likely. They would have booked me out for three-years' worth of six-month incremental appointments, had I let them. That strategy made me think.

I'm supporting a few people who have recently lost loved ones and I get sloppy in my actions on their behalf. Will I make my call, deliver the casserole and mail a card to those people who I pledged to support? Well, I always mean to. I do want to. But I wasn't being good about it.

To-do lists are fine, although they often get ignored, shuffled or redone, even though all their items weren't crossed off. Mine do. Only when we put tasks on our calendars do they become a real to-do item. Then they have become an appointment with time. If it shows up on Tuesday at 10:00 to be done then, well then by golly, I need to do it then. I've made an appointment and a commitment. Just like my planning and commitment to the dentist's office.

As soon as I got in my car after the dentist appointment, I entered those three things I've been meaning to do into my phone's calendar. And they are now done. It works!

What three-month or six-month action do you wish your supporters would put on their calendars? We appreciate the Calm After the Storm text that asks, "How are you doing *today*?" Or that invitation to go to a movie or golfing or to grab a cup of coffee *a few months* after the funeral. We'd value this more than clean teeth! Our supporters will feel good about offering this ongoing support. Everyone wins!

Chapter 10

Operation Shock & Awww

From Shock to 'Awww'

Operation Shock and Awe is a testosterone-laden, military-based concept that describes the overwhelming use of force at the beginning of a military conflict. It is intended to debilitate the enemy's will, spirit and functionality.

The term gained broad use in 2003 when the United States invaded Iraq during The Second Persian Gulf War (Operation Desert Storm). The U.S. Military stormed Iraq with a huge amount of force and armament, overwhelming the opponent.

Death feels like that kind of shock-filled assault. There are no bombs, tanks or missiles, but it feels like it. Our lives are emotionally blown up and altered in what feels like an irreparable way.

Death of loved ones can alter us even more than if we lost our health, jobs, incomes, investments, homes or anything else. We can recover from most of those losses. But death is not just a shock—it is *the* shock. One with no recovery or return of the person we lose, who is now gone forever.

We wander around in shock for X amount of time after the death of our loved ones. And as we have seen, there are various types of male mourning. We avoid the topic. We cry a lot inwardly and/or outwardly. We are paralyzed with fear, depression or bargaining. We move forward quickly in ways some might think odd. It's all an outgrowth of shock.

During my short-lived career in the Boy Scouts of America, I was tasked with creating a presentation for a community health fair. For some reason, I landed on the topic of shock. As a disconnected 13-year-old, I didn't know squat about shock. But I studied up on it in the Boy Scout book and from other sources.

I may have been in a pre-shock myself since this was the window of time when my mother was dying from breast cancer. I wasn't sure she was dying, but I did know that things were not right. Mom's illness was my first exposure to a slow death process. I wasn't in shock yet because she was still alive. But I felt quite lost the time I once asked what she needed when she was moaning in pain. She replied, "To die." That shocked me.

For my Boy Scout presentation's poster, I drew a figure lying on the ground with his feet propped up on a backpack. I explained to the not-so-interested health fair patrons that shock is caused when the blood rapidly drains out of one's head. That condition could be caused by any number of exciting or traumatic things. With too little blood flow to the head, the victim can become irrational. They should be treated for shock and allowed to recover.

The treatment for shock is to follow my poster's directions: Have the afflicted person lie down on their back and then position their feet onto something that is about 12 inches off the ground. The theory is that this action would help drain blood back to the person's brain. Then they'd recover their faculties. I didn't ever field test this solution on an actual shock victim so I can't tell you if it works. It seems to make sense in theory.

My wish for myself and you is that our grief shock dissipates. Let's hope that the blood drains back into our heads so we can eventually recover our faculties, like the person on my poster.

* * *

May your shock be replaced by Awww.

My favorite thought about *awww* is about babies. Yes, new puppies and kitties score high, but *babies t*op the Awww Chart. Carl Sandburg had it right when he stated that, "A baby is God's opinion that life should go on." Who doesn't go "Awww" when they see a new baby? Newborns and infants provoke a response of love, protection, nurture, hope and potential all rolled into a baby bundle of joy.

You may also feel *awww* when seeing a beautiful sunset, a mountain view, an ocean beach view, a field full of bounteous crops at sunrise, a lovely art creation, a finely-restored automobile, a well-written poem or story, or a breathtaking sculpture. Or any other number of *awww*-filled experiences that you appreciate.

Those are just some examples of the *awww* we all eventually hope to feel again. I hope you will move toward your *awww* and get beyond the shock part with regard to your lost loved one. Can you look at a photograph of your departed loved one and have an *Awww* reflection, instead of a tear-filled reaction?

***

Part of *awww* is spirituality. Spirituality means "being about the spirit or soul." I have found the death of loved ones really opens the door for personal spiritual growth. During this time, I've read more, prayed more and listened more than ever before in my life.

There are hundreds of faiths, religions, denominations and faith-related practices in the world. Each one has its own traditions regarding death, dying, grief and public mourning. No matter what your faith expression looks like, we can use this unique time in our lives to be more open than ever to communication with our God.

The theme of "God is with us" pervades most all religions and belief systems. I encourage you to be as open as possible so you can learn and grow all you can during this vulnerable, spirit-filled time. Here's a simple, comforting reminder:

God is our refuge and strength, an ever-present help in trouble.

Psalm 46:1
(New International Version of the Holy Bible)

Chapter 11
Does Grief Ever End?

Losing loved ones changes us forever. I know men whose loved ones died decades ago and others who have lost a loved one just months ago. Both groups have members who appear to be living normal-looking lives today. I also know that they still have their loved ones in their hearts. They just got used to their loss.

But I also know from chats with numerous mourning men that all this encouragement about moving from shock to *awww* may fall flat. "Just more platitudes," they might say. If you're still in raw shock, all of the concepts in this book can appear as gibberish to you. It will make no sense in your world. "I'm not ready for that kind of thinking," you protest. To those of you who feel that way, I say, "I get it, I understand, tell me more, I've been there, done that and I'm being there and am doing that."

* * *

When my adult daughter and my wife of 40 years died within nine months of each other, a friend who sees plenty of death in his work, called me "strong." Thanks for the compliment, *but I've never felt weaker in my life!* Never more confused, vulnerable or alone. That's what death does to the survivors. Even men. But we need to remember that while it is a very unusual feeling to be this out of control and vulnerable, it is normal. I keep repeating the word *normal* a lot but just know that your journey here is unique. Vulnerability is abnormal for lots of guys, but it's OK right now.

So, guys, what are we going to do about all of this? Guys like to do stuff, not just talk about it. One answer is a favorite story that comes from author Sharon Zehnder. Her grief-support book is, *CrossWords for Grief: God's Truths for Encouragement and Hope*. It incorporates survey-based grief topics with daily living stories with comforting, well-researched scriptures.

In her chapter on tears, Sharon recalls her mother's pressure cooker in her childhood home. In case you don't know what one is, they are large, sealable metal pots that steam vegetables under high pressure for canning to consume at a later time. The cooked vegetables are typically saved in sealed glass jars. The cookers have a pressure release valve on the top or side in order to release the steam pressure that builds up from the boiling contents. Without that release valve, the sealed cooker could explode.

Sharon makes the analogy about how tears are like the pressure release valve on those devices. Sometimes guys need a release valve of our own to let our own pressure and stressors out during the intense emotions surrounding death.

If we don't have or cultivate some form of positive outlet, we might blow up some other way, possibly in a negative fashion involving drugs, alcohol, sex, food extremes, held anger, ongoing depression, dangerous activities, etc. What's your pressure release valve? As mentioned, several times here, if grief isn't acknowledged, it is likely to hunt you down and eventually come out in some form.

What will you do? Exercise, meditate, pray, yell, seek fellowship, study the scriptures, find solitude, take nature hikes, or take up art, reading, painting, construction, paintball, demolition derbies, golfing, bicycling. Even grief groups are among the possibilities. How will you release your pressure?

* * *

One pressure release tool I'm learning more about is meditation. I used to think of it as a hobby for folks who wore tight pants, ate grass and spent money on candles. Recently, however, I'm learning that simple breathing in through the nose and exhaling through the mouth can be a tool to quiet a noisy mind. What mourning man doesn't need to quiet his noisy mind?

It takes practice. You didn't master your computer, mechanical skills, athletic or professional talent in just a day. The same goes for meditation. Simple, disciplined breathing exercises are really the basis of this easy way to calm our churning brains.

One key I've read about is to focus on the breathing only. Just focus on the *sound* of your breath. Listen to *it only* while trying to screen out other thoughts. When your next errand or some task you forgot to do jump into your mind, simply say, "OK" and start over.

Another technique is to come up with a neutral phrase that you can repeat with each breath. The phrase should be something simple and generic that keeps you focused on clearing your mind, not something like, "Take those boxes to Goodwill."

One that works for me is to think of the word "relax" as I inhale through my nose. Then I think "now" as I exhale. To use one or just a couple of repetitive words calms the brain I believe, because you don't need to be struggling to come up with something new. Some folks just moan or hum but I need more red meat to chomp onto than that. So simple is better, I feel. The goal is to have a "blank mind." I've been accused of having that in the past, but it wasn't due to meditation!

I'm eager to get better at it. My mind has always been a noisy and rapidly shifting place. That got worse after my daughter's and my wife's deaths. So, I'm eager to keep trying to set aside 10 minutes a day to work on improving this important technique. I can't report amazing results at this early phase, but I'm still learning and practicing. I've even kept Laura's yoga mat just in case I jump into this real deep. But don't expect to see me in yoga pants!

✶✶✶

Here's another type of pressure release valve: Find Your Marge. Recall Marge from the introduction in this book. She's the person I met at a grief group whose husband had recently died in a location apart from her. She was distraught that he died that way. She happened to tell me her story, and I was consoled when I saw her calm down after venting with me. It was rewarding to me to be helpful to her. That was one inspiration for this book and it evokes a call to action for Mourning Men:

Who can you help?

Maybe as a listener.

Maybe with a spontaneous dinner drop-off. Maybe replacing someone's furnace filter. Maybe watching their kids for a few hours. Or taking their car for an oil change.

Or going golfing or biking with them. Or a note in the mail.

Even just a "How are you doing, *today*?" text. Or any way to show you care.

You have something to offer. You're still here for a reason and your new or refined purpose is under construction. If you are ready for it, helping someone else even in a small way will honor your loved one's memory, and may help your healing.

* * *

If you are early in your grief journey, you may feel this terrible feeling of sadness will never go away. I still have daily waves of sadness so I can't testify that those feelings do, in fact, go away. Millions of Mourning Men have gone on to live semi-normal looking lives after their losses. They did so, most likely, by checking their emotional dipsticks along the way. Perhaps they also became a little more focused on *other* people in their lives instead of their own grief.

you how long it takes until we get used to
e yet. Even 12 months after the death of my
onths after the death of my daughter, I still
ngs that make me say to myself, "I've got to
tell Lisa about this." And I still have daily
TEARS Moments for Laura.

I hope we are all on the Keepers track; moving slowly toward finding meaning, positive reflections and some form of acceptance. It helps me to recall the words from Lady GaGa's performance of the song, "Always Remember Us This Way." This song became well-known from the 2018 movie, *A Star Is Born*. In this wistful tune, GaGa pays tribute to her dead lover. Verse two ends with this line:

"The part of you that's me will never die."

Daughter Laura also reminded us that we are:

"More Than This Body, More Than This Mind."

＊ ＊ ＊

Peace to all Mourning Men!

Appendix

NeverGrieveAlone.com Retreats

Guys, Never Grieve Alone

NeverGrieveAlone.com hosts retreats which provide support for men who have lost loved ones to death. They ensure that men never have to grieve alone.

Our weekend retreats are for men who have lost a spouse, child, sibling, parent or good friend. The only men attending these retreats are men who have been through that and relate to what you are going through.

The relaxed events are a mix of social and practical activities and reflection. Participants experience support while they deal with memories, sadness and grief. The events are based on Christian faith principles, but all faiths are welcome and should feel comfortable attending.

The retreats run from Saturday morning to Sunday noon. They are held several times a year in a variety of states at modern retreat center facilities.

Please see NeverGrieveAlone.com/retreats to learn current locations and schedules.

Call for Contributors

I Need Your Help with Two New Books:

Widower Reinvented and *Widow Power*

Becoming a widower or a widow changes a person's life. Widowers and widows want to, or are forced to reconfigure their existence. Not only emotionally reimagining themselves without their spouse, they often need to make financial, occupational or residential changes as well.

Widower Reinvented and the separate title, *Widow Power,* are my two new books in process. But these books need your help. Your true stories of widows and widowers who've made successful occupational transitions will inspire and assist others. Your story can help and inspire others.

What good work- or business-related transitions did you navigate after your loved one's death? Did you change jobs, get a new job or launch a business? Did you close a business, relocate or remarry? Did you set up a cause in the name of your dead child? What worked for you? What didn't work for you? What did you learn along the way?

Help me to help others via your story. You don't need to be a writer because we'll interview you and build the story. Interviews are usually done by phone or remote chat. If you have a post-death, reinvention story of job, career or entrepreneurial success, I want to hear it!

Three benefits of sharing your story:

1. It is helpful to other widowers and widows—they may get hope, inspiration and guidance from *you*.
2. If your reinvention involves a new or growing business or a job that benefits from networking and visibility, placement in these books can give you organic exposure in an evergreen, ongoing fashion.
3. Getting your story out into the public is often a great way to heal and continue your journey in a positive way.

These two books will be compilations of short success stories of you and others. You'll have final approval of the story before we publish them. This can be a fast, fun, healing process.

Please go to www.NeverGrieveAlone.com to learn how to contribute your story.

Acknowledgments

I hated writing this book. I hate that life handed me, my sons and Laura's fiancé, Kevin, the experiences behind this book. We'd all prefer a healthy wife, daughter, sister and fiancée. And to know no grief. But life is what happens to you when you are making other plans. So it goes. Death, they say, is a part of life.

The friends, family, neighbors, coworkers, business friends, online pals, bicycling buddies, church people and even strangers who supported me, my sons and Kevin through the deaths of Laura and Lisa all had a part in birthing this book. Their actions, words, inactions, silence, hugs, food, yard work, lodging, gift cards, golf games, bike rides, deck rebuilding and even *more* food made us feel lots of love. Saying "thank you" doesn't cover it, but *thank you*!

Special thanks to John and Lori Berglund for their early encouragement of this concept. Your positive responses after that August bike ride propelled this idea. As did that of Robert Hilkemann, who listened well to my lamentations and ranting while on a hike. I exclaimed, "I should write a book about this," and he encouraged me to do so. A shout out also to author and ghostwriter Kathy Rygg for our inspired title, content and proofing sessions, and to Kim Spillers for her over-the-top proofing work.

Sons Dane and Jake were huge contributors to this project. Dane will tell you in just a few words what he thinks of an idea. When he seemed comfortable with this theme, I knew I had something worthwhile. Son Jake offered his ongoing, silent support and let me ignore him while he was home on college breaks. As I hovered over the omnipresent keyboard, he'd say, "Done yet?" And I'd say, "Nope." Kevin's tireless, loving and informed caregiving of Laura is also a huge part of this story.

Major kudos to my Beta Reviewers. Many really talented people helped to rehab this content and make it exponentially better. In random order, a thousand thank you shout-outs go to: Dane Madsen, Lori Bergland, John Bergland, Julie Hilkemann, Robert Hilkemann, Beth Olson, Doug Sasse, "Red Pen" Jackie, author Joyce Brown, Ralph Orsi, author Sharon Zehnder, Andy Johnson, author Kathy Rygg and Angel-on-Earth, Kim Spillers. Your ideas, title, content and cover consultations, critiques, proofing, editing were priceless.

Thanks also to Frank Spillers for his title work, to Monica Sempek Photography, and to Lisa Pelto and Concierge Publishing Services for your skilled work and contributions. Thanks also to Jeff Quandt for your decade of technical and marketing support. The support all of you have shown to my family and this project communicates your love, and the "Mad Men" are ever-so-grateful. Your amazing work will help many people.

Laura Madsen and Lisa Madsen made the world a better place for the people in their lives.

There is a saying that goes: "They say a person dies twice. Once when you take your last breath, and then again when someone says your name for the last time." So, this content is a way for a small part of their stories to linger on. My hope is that this book allows Laura's and Lisa's lives *and deaths* to keep teaching and inspiring us all. Thanks for everything, "LAM" and "Lees." We'll see you on the other side.

About the Author

After graduating from Dana College and serving as a youth minister, Paul Madsen transitioned into the staffing/recruiting/placement industry. He focused primarily on hiring technology and healthcare talent. He worked for decades in that line of work, hiring/placing more than 1,000 people along the way.

Paul is the proud father of three: two adult sons, Dane and Jake, and his daughter, Laura, who died in 2020 due to long-term heart and lung issues. Paul's wife of 40 years, Lisa, died in 2021 due to complications from 50-plus years of juvenile diabetes.

Madsen, founder of growmedia.com, has written five books. He is passionate about supporting and promoting authors, small businesses and grief community providers via a TV talk show and social media videos. He serves grieving men through retreats (NeverGrieveAlone.com/retreats) in locations around the US. He enjoys writing, bicycling, golfing, water sports and traveling. Paul is a Wisconsin native currently residing in Nebraska.

* * *

Here's a link to Laura's two-minute motivation video:

https://www.youtube.com/watch?v=tEdDfSCQYYo&t=5s
"Laura's Auras" video

Made in the USA
Coppell, TX
17 September 2022

83264779R00063